M000023292

The Day of Baptism

____

child of

____

____

was baptized

on ______________________________
(date)

at ______________________________________
(church, city)

by ______________________________________
(pastor)

The Baptism of Your Child

The Baptism of Your Child

A Book for Presbyterian Families

Carol A. Wehrheim

© 2006, 2018 Westminster John Knox Press

Second edition
Published by Westminster John Knox Press
Louisville, Kentucky

18 19 20 21 22 23 24 25 26 27—10 9 8 7 6 5 4 3 2 1

All rights reserved. No part of this book may be reproduced or transmitted in any form or by any means, electronic or mechanical, including photocopying, recording, or by any information storage or retrieval system, without permission in writing from the publisher. For information, address Westminster John Knox Press, 100 Witherspoon Street, Louisville, Kentucky 40202-1396. Or contact us online at www.wjkbooks.com.

Unless otherwise indicated, Scripture quotations are from the New Revised Standard Version of the Bible, copyright © 1989 by the Division of Christian Education of the National Council of the Churches of Christ in the U.S.A., and are used by permission.

Stanzas from Ronald S. Cole-Turner, "Child of Blessing, Child of Promise," ©1981 Ronald S. Cole-Turner. All rights reserved. Used by permission.

Book design by Allison Taylor
Interior illustrations: © 2005 John Foster
Cover design by Lisa Buckley Design

Library of Congress Cataloging-in-Publication Data
Names: Wehrheim, Carol A., author.
Title: The baptism of your child : a book for Presbyterian families / Carol A. Wehrheim.
Description: Louisville, KY : Westminster John Knox Press, 2018. | Previously published: Louisville, Ky. : Geneva Press, c2006. |
Identifiers: LCCN 2017049236 (print) | LCCN 2017049370 (ebook) | ISBN 9781611648539 (ebk.) | ISBN 9780664263942 (pbk. : alk. paper)
Subjects: LCSH: Baptism--Presbyterian Church. | Christian education of children. | Presbyterian Church--Doctrines.
Classification: LCC BX9189.B3 (ebook) | LCC BX9189.B3 W44 2018 (print) | DDC 265/.12--dc23
LC record available at https://lccn.loc.gov/2017049236

PRINTED IN THE UNITED STATES OF AMERICA

♾ The paper used in this publication meets the minimum requirements of the American National Standard for Information Sciences—Permanence of Paper for Printed Library Materials, ANSI Z39.48-1992.

Most Westminster John Knox Press books are available at special quantity discounts when purchased in bulk by corporations, organizations, and special-interest groups. For more information, please e-mail SpecialSales@wjkbooks.com.

Contents

Baptizing Your Child

Child of blessing, child of promise,

Baptized with the Spirit's sign,

With this water God has sealed you

Unto love and grace divine.

—Ronald S. Cole-Turner, "Child of Blessing, Child of Promise"

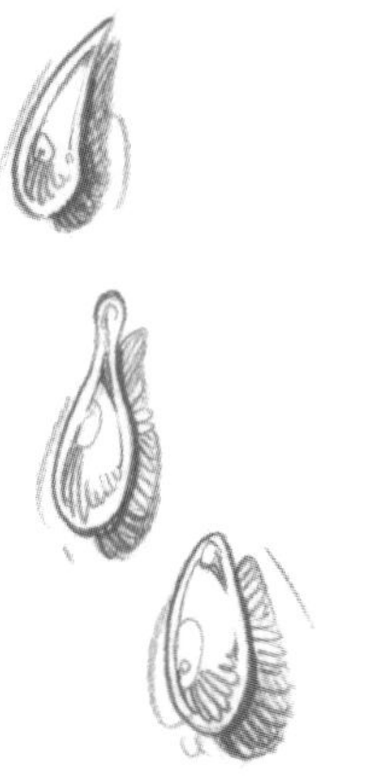

Congratulations!

You have begun a wonderful and exciting journey with your child. You began that journey long before this moment, but the day of your child's baptism will announce to the world and your church family that this journey is under way and that they are included.

As you prepare for your child's baptism, think about the family members and friends you want to be with you and your child, not only at the baptism but during the following years. Invite them in plenty of time so that they can make arrangements to be present. What memories do you want to provide for your child about this day? The stories you tell and the pictures you enjoy over and over will become your child's own when they are incorporated into your child's memory.

In this book you will find information and help as you parent your child for the years ahead. Keep it in a place where you will remember to refer to it often, and make it an active part of your role as the faith nurturer of your child.

May the baptism of your child rekindle your own faith, and may it be a day of great joy for you, your family, and your congregation. God's blessings on your family.

A Prayer for the Family

Loving God, who created families to nurture faith,
    send your Spirit now to this family.
Give the adults in this child's life the wisdom and courage
    to be models of faithful living.
Remind the congregation to enfold this child
    into their loving arms.
May the occasion of this child's baptism
    be a moment for all your people to remember your grace,
        freely given to all who know you.
In Christ's name. Amen.

Questions and Answers about Baptism

Q. Just what is baptism?

A. Baptism is a sacrament of the Christian church. In the Protestant and Reformed traditions, baptism is one of two sacraments. The other is Communion, also known as the Eucharist and the Lord's Supper. For these congregations, the sacraments are those instituted by Jesus through his own baptism (Luke 3:21–22) and through his words at the Last Supper, before he was arrested in the garden (22:14–20).

Baptism today is how the church follows Jesus' commission to the disciples to "Go therefore and make disciples of all nations, baptizing them in the name of the Father and of the Son and of the Holy Spirit, and teaching them to obey everything that I have commanded you" (Matt. 28:19–20). A sacrament is a sign and symbol of God's love and mercy. It is a means of grace, a way that we receive God's love that is freely given, based on nothing that we have done to earn it. In baptism, we begin a new life with Christ.

Q. What happens during a baptism?

A baptism typically has these elements: Presentation of the Baptismal Candidate, Profession of Faith, Thanksgiving over the Water, The Act of Baptism, and Welcome. The ritual for a service of baptism is on pages 10–14. The words may vary from pastor to pastor, but the meaning will be much the same. The pastor asks parents and others present to commit to teach and model the Christian faith for the child and dabs or pours a small amount of water on the child's forehead.

Sometimes children in the congregation are invited to sit near the baptismal font for an infant baptism. They may be asked a question, such as, "Will you be a friend to (*child*) and help him/her learn about Jesus?" Your older children may be invited to stand with you for the service of baptism. Even though the child to be baptized may be asleep or noisily complaining about this disruption of the morning routine, this is an important moment for your whole family and for the congregation.

Q. Why can't I just wait and let my child decide about being baptized in the church?

A. Of course, that is an option, and some churches in other denominations require that persons to be baptized make their own profession of faith. This is often called believer's baptism, or simply adult baptism. Most of those churches have a dedication service for new babies and young children to remind parents and the congregation that this child is to be nurtured in God's love and ways. However, infant baptism reminds us that God has given us the gift of love and grace even before we ask. In the Reformed tradition, of which the Presbyterian Church (U.S.A.) is a part, baptism is a sign of our covenant with God, a covenant that includes all generations. The baptism of your child—of any child, no matter how young—reminds the congregation of God's grace and covenant in Jesus the Christ.

Some traditions, including the Roman Catholic Church, believe that baptism is necessary for salvation. Churches in the Reformed tradition understand the sacrament of baptism as a symbol of that salvation by God but not that the sacrament bestows it upon us. While Presbyterians do not equate the sacrament of baptism with being saved, you are encouraged to present your child for baptism "without undue delay." Your child may not remember this occasion, but you can make that memory live for and in your child by celebrating her or his baptism day annually.

Q. Can we baptize our baby with just our family at home or in the church?

A. In the Reformed tradition, baptism is understood to be an act of the congregation. The congregation is the corporate sponsor of your child. When the congregation gathers around the baptismal font, every member is reminded of her or his baptism and the ever-present mercy and love of God. Baptism is not between you and God; it is an important occasion for the church, for you, and for your child as everyone acknowledges that God has joined us together through Jesus Christ. Just as you make promises about how you will raise your child in the faith, so does the congregation promise to care for your child's spiritual growth.

Q. Do I find a godparent or sponsor for my child?

A. In the Presbyterian Church (U.S.A.) the entire congregation agrees to nurture the baptized child in the faith. In essence, the congregation as a whole takes on the role of godparent or sponsor. A session (the ruling body of the congregation) may name some people as sponsors, to take special responsibility for that nurture. In some congregations, an elder takes part in the baptism and then maintains contact with the baptized child and family through such things as cards on birthdays and baptism anniversaries. Or a deacon may be assigned to your family before and after the baptism. If you would like a sponsor for your child and family, speak to your pastor about that possibility. And yes, sometimes parents ask close friends or family members to stand with them during the baptism.

Q. Is the water used in baptism special in some way?

A. The water in the baptismal font is ordinary tap water. However, it does have a symbolic meaning: the waters of creation (Gen. 1:1–4), the flood (6:5–9:17), and the water that flowed from the rock during the exodus (Exod. 17:1–7). Thus, this water connects us to the covenants in the Hebrew Scriptures with Noah and the people of Israel. God's prophets talked of the waters of righteousness and gave God's people the hope of a new covenant (Amos 5:23–25). Jesus spoke of himself as living water and encouraged the Samaritan woman at the well to accept the water of everlasting life (John 4:4–15). The water that will be used to baptize your child is ordinary water, but it is water full of symbolic meaning.

Q. How much water is needed to baptize?

A. In the Reformed tradition, baptism can be done by pouring, sprinkling, or immersion (dipping the person into water). Water is the visible sign for this sacrament, just as the cup and bread are the visible signs for Communion. Therefore, water should be used so that it can be seen, even generously. Pastors have their own ways of holding the infant, often depending on the size of the child and how fretful the baby is. Therefore, whether the water is poured or sprinkled may depend on several factors unrelated to our understanding of baptism.

Q. A friend in a different Presbyterian congregation says that babies there are anointed with oil during the baptism. Should I expect that?

A. The services for the sacrament of baptism in our *Book of Common Worship* do include an anointing with oil (making the sign of the cross on the forehead) following the baptism with water, with these words:

> (*Name*), child of the covenant,
>
> you have been sealed by the Holy Spirit in baptism,
>
> and marked as Christ's own forever. **Amen.**

However, our *Book of Order* specifies that when anointing with oil is included in the sacrament of baptism, it should be explained and should not overshadow the central act of baptizing with water.

Q. I've noticed that the pastor uses only the given names during baptisms and not the family name. Why is that?

A. First, the pastor didn't forget to say the family name. Using just the given names or Christian name emphasizes that baptism symbolizes becoming part of another family, the family of God. The child now has the name "Christian" as well. The baptized child has been adopted into the covenant family of the church. And that is not only the congregation where your child is baptized, but the church universal. Baptism is not into a denomination but into the church of Jesus Christ.

Emphasizing the adoption into the family of God doesn't mean that you relinquish your parental responsibilities for nurturing your child in the faith. However, it does mean that the congregation has important responsibilities too, as you can see when you read the promises made by the congregation at a baptism. And should you move and become part of a different congregation, they take up that vow.

Q. My wife is not a member of any church. If we have our child baptized, what is her role in the baptism?

A. Because you are the member, you are the one who makes the promises at the baptism. If your wife is supportive of this act and wishes to, she can stand with you as your child is baptized. Suggest that she accompany you to the education about baptism or meeting with your pastor so that you have a common understanding of this sacrament.

When parents are of different faith traditions, they have to decide where their baby will be baptized. This may not be an easy conversation. You may have thought religious decisions were settled by now. However, it is helpful to remember that the question is not which is the better congregation in which to raise your child but how you can nurture yourselves and your child in its faith community and participate in it fully.

Q. What does baptism mean for children with birth defects or serious illness?

A. The important thing to remember is that baptism is not about who we are or what we can do. Baptism is God's gift of grace and mercy to us. We do nothing to earn it. Every child, whatever its health, whatever its station in life, whatever its capabilities, is the recipient of that wondrous grace and mercy.

If you have additional questions about baptism or are unclear about an answer here, please speak with your pastor. She or he will welcome your interest.

A Service for Infant Baptism[1]

A presider may open with a litany drawn from Scripture.

Elder or session-appointed sponsor:

On behalf of the session, I present (*Name*), child of (*Name*) and (*Name*), to receive the Sacrament of Baptism.

Minister (to parents):

Do you desire that (*Name*) be baptized? **I do.**

Relying on God's grace,
do you promise to live the Christian faith,
and to teach that faith to your child? **I do.**

Minister (to sponsors, if any are present):

Will you, by your prayers and witness, help (*Name*) to grow into the full stature of Christ? **I will.**

1. A variety of services for the sacrament of baptism are available. If the questions above are not those usually used by your pastor, they will be questions with similar content and intent.

Minister (to congregation):

Do you, as members of the church of Jesus Christ,
promise to guide and nurture (*Name*)
by word and deed,
with love and prayer? **We do.**

Will you encourage them to know and follow Christ and to be faithful members of his church? **We will.**

Profession of Faith

Through the Sacrament of Baptism we enter the covenant
God established in Jesus Christ.

Within this covenant God gives us new life,
strengthens us to resist evil,
and nurtures us in love.

Through this covenant, we choose whom we will serve,
by turning from evil and turning to Jesus Christ.

The presider asks the following questions of the candidates for baptism and/or the parents or guardians of children being presented for baptism.

Trusting in the gracious mercy of God,
do you turn from the ways of sin
and renounce evil and its power in the world? **I renounce them.** or **I do.**

Who is your Lord and Savior? **Jesus Christ is my Lord and Savior.**

Will you be Christ's faithful disciple,
obeying his word and showing his love? **I will, with God's help.**

The people may stand.

With the whole church,
let us confess our faith.

I believe in God, the Father almighty,
creator of heaven and earth.

I believe in Jesus Christ, God's only Son, our Lord,
who was conceived by the Holy Spirit,
born of the Virgin Mary,
suffered under Pontius Pilate,
was crucified, died, and was buried;
he descended to the dead.
On the third day he rose again;
he ascended into heaven,

The Apostles' Creed is the oldest statement of belief of the Christian church. In saying it together, we remember the long history of the church of Jesus Christ and Jesus' commission to the disciples to baptize in the name of the Father, and of the Son, and of the Holy Spirit.

he is seated at the right hand of the Father,
and he will come to judge the living and the dead.

I believe in the Holy Spirit,
the holy catholic church,
the communion of saints,
the forgiveness of sins,
the resurrection of the body,
and the life everlasting. Amen.

Thanksgiving over the Water

During the prayer of thanksgiving over the water, biblical references to water may be included, such as the waters of creation (Gen. 1:1–4), the flood (6:5–9:17), and the water that flowed from the rock during the exodus (Exod. 17:1–7).

The Lord be with you. **And also with you.**

Let us give thanks to the Lord our God. **It is right to give our thanks and praise.**

The Baptism

(*Name*), I baptize you
in the name of the Father,
and of the Son,
and of the Holy Spirit. **Amen.**

Welcome

The newly baptized is presented to the congregation and welcomed into Christ's church.

—From *Book of Common Worship* (Louisville, KY: Westminster John Knox Press, 2018), 408–11.

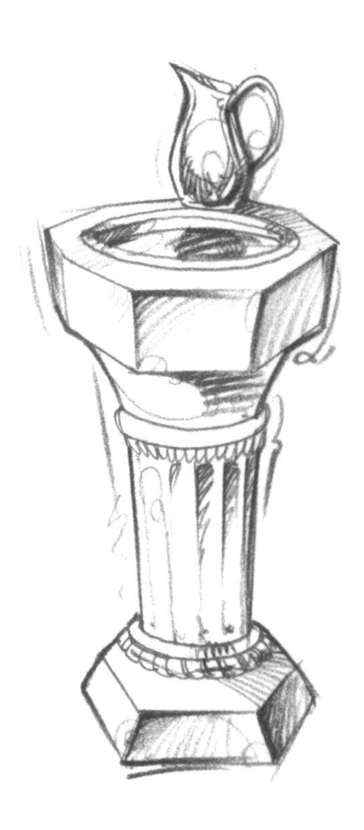

Catechism Questions on Baptism

Question 71. What is baptism?

Baptism is the sign and seal through which we are joined to Christ.

Question 72. What does it mean to be baptized?

My baptism means that I am joined to Jesus Christ forever. . . . As I am baptized with water, he baptizes me with his Spirit, washing away all my sins and freeing me from their control. My baptism is a sign that one day I will rise with him in glory, and may walk with him even now, in newness of life.

Question 73. Are infants also to be baptized?

Yes. Along with their believing parents, they are included in the great hope of the gospel and belong to the people of God. Forgiveness and faith are both promised to them . . . through Christ's covenant with his people.

—From *The Study Catechism*, copyright 1998 Geneva Press. All rights reserved.

Book of Order Statements on Baptism

Statements from the introduction to the Service of Baptism in the Directory for Worship in the *Book of Order*:

> The Reformed tradition understands Baptism to be a sign of God's covenant. . . . Like circumcision, a sign of God's gracious covenant with Israel, Baptism is a sign of God's gracious covenant with the Church.
>
> When we are baptized, we are made one with Christ, with one another, and with the Church of every time and place.
>
> The baptism of our young children witnesses to the truth that God claims people in love even before they are able to respond in faith.

—From *The Constitution of the Presbyterian Church (U.S.A.)*, Part II, *Book of Order* (Louisville, KY: Office of the General Assembly, Presbyterian Church (U.S.A.), 2017), W-3.0402.

A Partner for the Journey

Child of love, our love's expression,

Love's creation, loved indeed!

Fresh from God, refresh our spirits;

Into joy and laughter lead.

—Ronald S. Cole-Turner, "Child of Blessing, Child of Promise"

The Congregation's Promise

Remember the promise the congregation makes during the sacrament of baptism? The congregation promises at each and every baptism to guide and nurture the child by word and deed, with love and prayer, so that the child might come to follow Jesus Christ and be a faithful member of his church. This is said in different ways from congregation to congregation, but it all adds up to the same thing: the congregation should be an active participant in providing spiritual nurture for your child. While no one can take your place, the congregation, together and individually, can and should play an important role in the development of your child's faith. As it takes a village to raise a child, it takes a congregation to raise a child in the faith.

Just as Anna took the baby Jesus and showed this tiny Messiah to all who were in the temple, the congregation, as the representative of the whole church, reaches out toward your child and recognizes that your child is a child of God, a child of the covenant. With a splash of water and a few words, the church accepts responsibility for your child, taking the child under its watch and care. Your child is now enrolled as a baptized member in the membership rolls.

With this stress on the congregation, however, we must not forget that the congregation is also the representative of the wider church, the whole people of God around the world. Wherever you live, the congregation of that place is prepared to carry out this promise, just as your congregation carries out the promise made by other congregations.

The Church as Godparent

Godparents or sponsors are not common in the Presbyterian Church (U.S.A.) because we understand the congregation to be corporate godparent. As you might imagine, some church members warm to that responsibility more easily than others. Some people find it natural to talk with children; others prefer to converse with young adults. The important thing is that you and your child are around the church so that the many "godparents" can get to know your family.

You may be close to certain church members, such that they become like family. You naturally want them to play an important role in your child's spiritual life. Begin immediately to include them in family times so that your child will know them as "special" family friends. If you are new to the congregation, look around for a single adult, a couple, or a family you think will mesh well with your family. It may take several tries, but the result will be worth it.

An elder who participates in your child's baptism may choose to take a more extensive role beyond the responsibilities on baptism day. In some congregations, the elders are encouraged to call the family the week before the baptism and to greet them at the church building, making them comfortable and being sure that everything is ready. Some elders maintain a contact with the child and family through birthday cards and notes commemorating the baptism anniversaries. These greetings might continue until the child begins Sunday school or until the child is confirmed.

What the Congregation Might Offer

The opportunities for the congregation to keep its baptismal promise to your child are seemingly endless, but each congregation has its own way to be faithful. What follows are some of the possibilities. You will not find all of them in your congregation, but those described will help you think about what your congregation does or might offer.

- **Photograph of your family taken on the baptism day.** One congregation takes and prints two photographs of parents and child on the baptism morning. One photo is displayed on a bulletin board featuring newly baptized children at the church. The other is given to the family and can be part of the celebration of the child's baptism each year.

- **Printed materials.** Your congregation has already given you this book, an initial step in being your partner in the faith nurturing of your child. Look through it and note the suggestions that you want to use. Perhaps you were given a first-year-of-life calendar when your child was born or adopted, a CD of church music, or a Bible storybook as a gift from the congregation. In a year or two, you may receive information about the church school.

- **Deacon assigned as a partner.** Some congregations assign a deacon to families with infants or as soon as the pregnancy or pending adoption is known. Adjusting to life with a new little family member takes time. The deacon can check in to see how things are going as well as to provide you with information about congregational life so that you will continue to feel included.

- **Support during difficult or stressful times.** Not every pregnancy or adoption goes smoothly. The first weeks, even months, with a newborn can be difficult. Post-partum depression is real, and care for the new mother is important. The church staff is there to help you and to tell you of other resources. Don't be afraid you'll be "taking up their time."

- **Child care.** Many churches provide child care for infants and toddlers during worship and other times when the congregation gathers. You may prefer to have your tiny baby with you, but take advantage of the nursery when you are ready to do so. This nursery is the first step toward your child's feeling welcome and at home in the church building without you.

- **Classes or fellowship times for parents.** As you are able, take advantage of gatherings of parents in your congregation. Learn from the experiences of others, and you will soon find that you are gaining and giving support as well. Parents in one congregation asked for a Bible study while their children were in choir rehearsal. This group has become a close fellowship group too.

- **Prayer.** Those congregations with prayer chains are openly ready to receive your requests for prayer support. But you can always ask one or two church members to pray for you and your family. And never doubt that there are members who are praying for all the children of the congregation, even without your asking.

- **Birthday or baptism day cards.** Some congregations have volunteers who send birthday cards to young children who have been baptized. Some churches also mark the baptism day anniversary with a note.

- **Sunday school classes.** As your child gets older, somewhere around age two or three, your congregation will probably provide a Sunday school class. For such young children, these informal times normally include a lot of play, a Bible story when children are ready to listen, and some kind of artwork to complete. This is another milestone as your child discovers a place in the faith community.

The congregation has not fulfilled the baptismal promise when your child leaves the infant and toddler stages. It continues to be your partner by providing educational opportunities, welcoming your child into the service of worship, presenting your child with a Bible, and offering fellowship groups and a confirmation class. Recognize that how you introduce your child to these "special friends" now can set the tone for how your child will participate in other church activities later on.

Your Role in the Partnership

Don't just sit back and wait for the congregation to act. If you need particular help or support, ask for it. Each family is unique. Don't expect others to guess what you need from the church. Here are some ways that you can assist the congregation in being your partner:

- Be present in worship and at other church activities as often as possible.
- Get to know families and adults in the congregation so that they can get to know you.
- Invite church members over for dessert or a meal.
- Look for single adults or couples without children who would cherish the chance to be included in your family life, and in your child's life. Your child may lead them into joy and laughter too.

What would you add to this list?

Your Role as Faith Nurturer

Child of joy, our dearest treasure,

God's you are, from God you came.

Back to God we humbly give you:

Live as one who bears Christ's name.

—Ronald S. Cole-Turner, "Child of Blessing, Child of Promise"

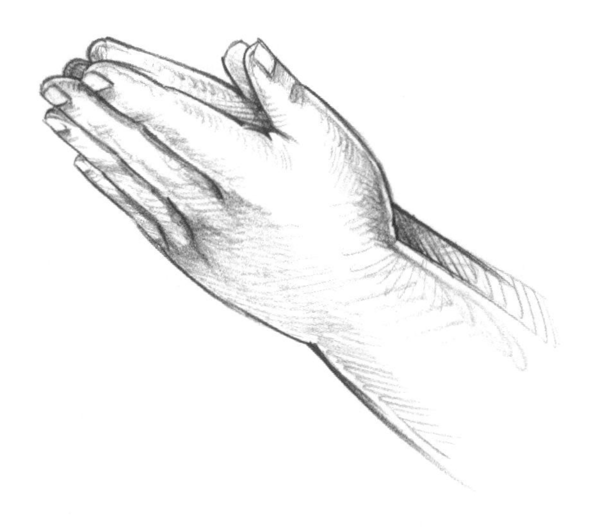

Your Promise

At your child's baptism, you promised to "live the Christian faith and to teach that faith to your child." Although the congregation is your partner in that role, you are the primary faith nurturer of your child, especially during the first years of life. But don't let that idea overwhelm you; rather, let it energize you. Parents have taken hold of this responsibility for generations upon generations. Moses admonished all the people, including the parents, after he had recited God's law to them: "Take to heart all the words that I am giving in witness against you today; give them as a command to your children, so they may diligently observe all the words of this law. *This is no trifling matter for you, but rather your very life*" (Deut. 32:46–47a, italics mine). Note the words in italics. We cannot keep God's word from our children. And Peter, on the day of Pentecost, said, "For the promise is for you, for your children, and for all who are far away, everyone whom the Lord our God calls" (Acts 2:39).

John Calvin wrote at length about what parents are to teach their children about faith. Just as you will be watching and looking after your child's physical, emotional, and social development over the years, so too can you look after your child's faith and spiritual development. Your child's spiritual development is important to her or his fulfillment of potential, success, and thriving. Spiritual development is as natural as physical and social development. Just as you encourage your child to take that first step or to wave good-bye, encourage your child to respond from the heart and to grow in her or his knowledge of God. Much of your nurturing and parenting role in these areas will come naturally. Other parts of it you will learn from many sources. Keep this book handy so that you can look over the suggestions here from time to time, selecting those that fit your child and you at the moment.

Martin Luther called the home "the domestic church." Your home is where your child will learn these foundations of faith: trust, wonder, and imagination. They are present in all thriving children, and according to developmental theorists, trust is the important issue for the young child to sort out. As your child learns that you, a person who can be seen, can be trusted for food, warmth, and all that is needed, then he or she will be able to trust God, who cannot be seen. Every time you go away from your child and return, trust is being built. You nurture these three developmental qualities by loving your children and providing an environment that is trustworthy and open to the child's wonder and imagination. Christian parents add a faith dimension to that loving as they live out their faith right before their children's eyes.

Current studies strongly indicate that adolescents who have a strong relationship with God and ties to adults in their religious communities are more able to meet life's challenges successfully. The first step to providing your child with the path to that success can be her or his baptism and your continued engagement with the congregation. So let's see how you might live out that faith during these first years together.

> I think families intentionally communicate the values and vision of faith in two basic ways. The first is through the *natural opportunities* of life together—occasions that simply characterize the relational fabric of family life. The second is through *intentional practices*—simple but specific structures and patterns that support the spiritual potential within families of faith.
>
> —From Marjorie J. Thompson, *Family—the Forming Center: A Vision of the Role of Family in Spiritual Formation* (Nashville: Upper Room Books, 1996), 21.

The First Year with Your Child

Emotions and actions, much more than words, are the language that convey meaning to infants. So how you touch, speak to, and care for your little one will make all the difference in the development of trust, resulting in both trusting you and trusting God. Showing your love invites your child to love. All the cooing, caressing, and cuddling you shower on your baby helps their development in all areas, including faith and spiritual development. Keep that in mind as you try some of the ideas below.

- **Pray for your child.** I am sure you already pray for your child, and did so long before this little one arrived in your home. Now, however, you can pray for your child aloud when you are holding your child or standing over the crib. Let the sound of your voice giving thanks to God and asking for God's love and care be among the earliest words that your child remembers.
- **Pray with your child.** Say a simple thank-you prayer when you feed your child—something like, "Thank you, God, for food that makes us grow." As your child notices new things like toes, say, "Thank you, God, for toes" or "Thank you, God, for sunshine" as your child watches a sunbeam flicker on the wall. In this way you are giving thanks and your child is hearing faith language as naturally as when you say, "What a strong baby!"

A Prayer in the Morning

Loving God, thank you for another day with (*child's name*). Keep us in your care each minute. Amen.

A Blessing at Night

(*Child's name*), may God bless and keep you now and forever. Amen.

- **Introduce your infant to the music of the church.** Sing or hum hymns or carols (yes, even out of season) as you cuddle or rock your child. One congregation gives a recording made by their children's choir as a baptismal gift, encouraging parents to play it so that the child grows up hearing the music of the church. Music is the earliest intelligence to be observed in children. You will see it in your baby when an arm and leg starts moving in rhythm to a song you are singing or playing.

- **Speak the Bible to your child.** Infants are not quite ready to listen to a story, but you can develop your child's faith vocabulary with simple Bible verses said rhythmically or with patty-cake motions. Look to the psalms for short verses or phrases (substituting "God" for "Lord"): "The earth is God's and all that is in it" (Ps. 24:1), "It is good to give thanks to God" (92:1), "God is good to all" (145:9), or "Praise God!" (150:1).

- **Recall your baby's baptism.** When you bathe your baby, pour some water over your child's head. Describe aloud something you remember about your child's baptism.

Your caring love is the first word of God's love to your child. Express it often and speak it aloud. How you live with and love your new child during this first year provides the important component of trust so basic to faith and spiritual development and a positive relationship with God.

Notes from the First Year with Your Child

Your Child's Faith Development through the Years

Ages 2–3

You must surely be amazed at the changes in your child as you recall how that tiny infant has grown. Now you probably have a child who speaks and mimics your words. Your child will also invite you to a renewed spirituality and faith as she or he develops. What a wondrous plan God has for our growth and development! Along with the activities that you continue from your child's first year, here are new ideas:

- **Pray together.** Now is the time to introduce mealtime prayers that your child can say with you. Snacks are meals too; invite your child to thank God then as well. You might begin mealtime prayers by inviting your child to repeat after you: "Thank you, God, for *(something you will eat)*. Amen." This not only encourages the child to thank God but attaches names to food items. Also begin the practice of blessing or prayer for the child on the child's first birthday.

Mealtime Prayers

God is great. God is good. And we thank God for this food. Amen.

Thank you, God, for this food and for our family. Amen.

God, we thank you for this day and for this food. Amen.

- **Celebrate your child's baptism anniversary.** Look at photographs from the day. Tell your child about the baptism day. Purchase a white pillar candle. On each baptism anniversary, light the candle and let it burn for a time, a reminder that Jesus is the light of the world and that God is present in your child's life. Invite a few family and friends for a party. Serve a special dessert and ask each person present to bless the child. If you are a distance from grandparents, get to know some older members of your congregation who may be willing to become special friends to your family. The value of multigenerational friendships for your child (and for you) can't be overestimated.

- **Read Bible storybooks to your child.** At different ages, children are ready to sit in your lap or snuggle with you while you read. Board books are easiest for their hands to turn, and they will want to turn the pages for you. (See the resources section at the end of this book for suggestions and help in selecting Bible storybooks.)

- **Model faithfulness.** Your child is a mimic of actions as well as words. If your child sees you fold your hands and bow your head when you pray, she or he will begin to do the same. But your child will accept other acts of faithfulness too. If going to church to learn about and to worship God has been a regular practice throughout your child's life, that pattern will be the norm later on. Don't underestimate the value of putting in place now what you want to be the faith practices of your family in the years to come. Studies show that adolescents who have a sustained relationship with a loving and guiding God are better able to withstand life's challenges. Begin building that sustained relationship now.

- **Talk together about how to discipline your child, who is now an explorer par excellence.** An important component of discipline is forgiveness. Now is when you begin to provide your child with experiences on which to base an understanding of God's grace and forgiveness as well as God's love and care.

You will surely be busy just keeping up with all the new things your child can say and do in these early years. Don't let this busyness keep you from stepping back from time to time to rejoice and delight in your child.

Ages 4–6

Until now, most likely you have been the one who began prayers or spoke of God. Perhaps your child has already reminded you of a missed mealtime prayer or has given thanks to God at the sight of a ladybug or a rainbow. Watch for those moments. Enjoy them with your child. Continue to nurture your child's faith, drawing from these suggestions.

- **Begin nighttime prayers to which your child contributes.** You have been praying aloud with your child. Now invite your child to join in those prayers by asking whom he or she would like God to bless. Explain that this is asking God to watch over the person, which is our acknowledgment that this is what God does. You might suggest siblings, grandparents, and friends. Soon your child will name people with little help from you.

- **Decorate a table or special place in the home with the current church-season color.** Hang ribbons of the color from the dining room chandelier, or display a felt banner featuring the color in the family room. With your child, look for those colors in the sanctuary too.

Church Season Colors

Advent: blue or purple

Christmas and Epiphany: white or gold

Ordinary Time from Epiphany to Lent: green

Lent: purple

Easter to Pentecost: white or gold

Pentecost: red

Ordinary Time from Pentecost to Advent: green

- **Teach politeness and kindness.** This is more than manners, of course. You are building an understanding in your child of how we treat one another because each person is a child of God. Need it be said that how you treat your child ought to reinforce this theological concept? Your model can be your most effective teaching tool. This is also another way that you help your child build a relationship with God.

- **Teach sharing and caring.** These acts are really the beginning of your child's stewardship education. How she or he learns to treat God's world, to share with others known and unknown, and to contribute to the church or community will be based on an understanding of caring and sharing. Be forewarned that sharing may not come easily for many children, but continue to look for ways to make this a natural part of living together.

- **Continue to celebrate your child's baptism anniversary.** As you do this year after year, you are creating memories of that day for your child to carry throughout life. Perhaps it seems like only yesterday you were holding an infant in your arms, wondering how you were going to manage. Now that child calls you by name and has a mind of her or his own, just the way God intended. Relax! You are doing a wonderful job of nurturing your child's faith and spiritual development.

Ages 7–12

Let's think about the years until your child is confirmed, taking the vows of baptism as her or his own. Your role as faith nurturer continues as you maintain some rituals and routines and begin some new ones appropriate to the growing faith of your child. During these years, take time to nourish your own faith too. But more about that later. Here are a few ideas for nurturing faith in your school-aged child.

- **Continue to celebrate the baptism anniversary.** Light the baptismal candle. Pray for your child. Look at the photographs and tell stories to reinforce your child's memory of that day. Continue any other traditions you have developed, such as inviting special friends outside the church.

- **Continue to pray with and for your child.** In a couple of years, introduce the spiritual practice of *examen*, as an advanced type of nighttime prayer. Include times for silence in prayer as well, helping your child understand that prayer includes listening for God's word to us, which builds your child's relationship with God.

Examen

Examen is prayed at the end of the day. You begin by reviewing the day's events with these two questions (or some variation of them):

1. When did I feel happy about things today? When was everything right in my day—a time when I felt sure of God's presence?
2. When did I feel sad about things today? When was my day upsetting, when I felt far away from God?

When you ask the first question, give thanks for those moments when all felt right and good.

When you ask the second question, ask God to help you make such times and relationships new.

- **Encourage your child's participation in Sunday school and other educational ministries.** Few young children can walk to church on their own; parents are responsible for getting their children there. Look for ways to support your child's participation: invite church friends to play, get to know other families in the church with a child at or near your child's age, and take an interest in what your child is learning.

- **Reclaim Sabbath time.** Although you felt busy with a toddler, you will feel just as busy with a ten-year-old in your home. Begin a practice as soon as you can of a Sabbath time for your family. Set aside a day or part of a day each week or on some regular basis. Use this time to grow together as a family and to nurture your faith together. One family set Friday night as a time when they ate together, played games, and had a time of prayer together, when each family member brought prayer concerns and joys. When and how you do this will depend on many things particular to your family: ages of children, work patterns of parents, children's outside activities, and more. But begin now!

- **Teach your children about stewardship.** You will be helping your child learn about money and how to manage it. Include learning about giving to others and the church. Usually this begins when a child receives an allowance. A successful method is to give the child four jars: one for giving money to the church, one for weekly expenses that you and your child have agreed will come out of the allowance, one for savings, and one for whatever the child wishes.

  But stewardship is about more than money. Consider how your family can live as stewards of all God's creation as well.

- **Participate in mission or service projects together.** Begin with including your child when you buy cans of food for a food pantry or sort clothing for a clothing drive. As you do this, tell your child what you are doing and why. As your child matures, work in a soup kitchen together or join in some other mission project that will interest your child. Keep your child's safety in mind, and be sure to talk with your child about what you are doing and who is being helped. Explain that you do this because you are disciples of Jesus the Christ.

- **Involve your child when your family practices the spiritual discipline of hospitality.** Children learn to be welcoming when they are welcomed, but they also learn how to be welcoming when we include them in times of hospitality. If you have found some church members who are becoming integrated into your family life, include your child when sending birthday greetings or other notes. Give your child tasks when guests are coming. Invite people of other ethnic groups and cultures to your home. If possible, host one or two young people when a college choir or some other group is on tour in your area. Get to know refugee families in your community.

- **Talk about matters of faith as the topics and questions arise.** Children often think about something they hear in worship and in church school a long time before the question is asked. And you are the most likely person to get the question. Don't panic! Treat a question as an opportunity for a conversation when you can learn more about your child's faith. Ask your child about her or his own ideas before you speak your own. This also helps you clarify what is behind the question. Be honest, and don't be afraid to say, "I don't know." Then continue the conversation and search for answers together.

- **Worship together with your congregation.** The worship of God is the act that binds us together as the body of Christ. Help your child participate in congregational worship. Teach your child responses used by your congregation. For example, does your congregation respond with "Thanks be to God" following Scripture reading when the reader says, "This is the word of God"? Practice it with your child.

  Some congregations provide worship bags for children with materials about worship along with paper and pencils. If yours doesn't, put together your own: bookmarks to mark the hymns, a copy of the Lord's Prayer, and anything else that would help your child participate in worship.

You will surely find other ways to nurture your child's faith and spiritual development during these years. If something doesn't work, try another idea. Just as each family is unique, so is each child. God planned it that way!

Nurturing Your Own Faith

The way you nurture your own faith is a powerful example to your child. For how can you nurture your child if you aren't growing in your own spiritual life? Here are some areas to consider.

- **Prayer.** When your child was an infant, you prayed aloud over that child. As your child grew, you prayed together. When does your child see you in prayer now? Have the adults take turns at mealtime prayer too. One woman described how shocked she was to hear her father pray on Thanksgiving when she was an adult. With a large family, children were always the ones to pray at mealtimes. On this occasion, however, for the first time in her memory she heard her father pray aloud.

  Work on other spiritual practices and talk about them with your child. Through example let your child know that seeking God through prayer and other practices, such as meditation or journaling, continues throughout life.

- **Bible reading.** Set aside a time, if only for ten minutes a week, to read the Bible on a regular basis. Use this time to meditate on it for your own growth. But however you choose to read the Bible, let your child see you reading it. Don't just read it when your child is asleep or not around. As your child gets older, read it together and talk about it.

- **Fellowship.** Include some members of your church in your sphere of friends. Let your child see that church is more than gathering on Sunday morning for worship. Look for ways to meet new people in your congregation. Find support for providing a Christian household through others in your church.

- **Bible study.** Participate in the adult education program of your congregation. Be a model of lifelong spiritual growth for your child. An excellent way to learn more about the Bible and the Christian faith is to volunteer to teach Sunday school.

  How you live out your faith and how you keep it alive will provide your child with models to follow into adulthood. Look over any reflections you recorded here or elsewhere to inform how you and your child have grown together in faith. You don't have to do everything all the time, but search for the pattern that is nourishing to you. That pattern will nourish your child's faith as well. But above all, trust in God's grace and know that God's Spirit will be present, working among you, whatever happens.

Memories of You and Your Child Growing Together in Faith

Resources for Understanding More about Baptism and Nurturing Your Child's Faith

Child of God, your loving Parent,

Learn to know whose child you are.

Grow to laugh and sing and worship;

Trust and love God more than all.

—Ronald S. Cole-Turner, "Child of Blessing, Child of Promise"

Selecting Bible Storybooks and Bibles for Children

Bible Storybooks for Toddlers

Look for board books with one simple storyline and uncluttered illustrations. Seek out appropriate stories (not every Bible story needs to be told to young children) and retellings that will not have to be untaught at an older age. Stories about God's creation and Jesus and the children are perfect for this age.

Bible Storybooks for Young Children

Young children, who are not yet reading, may be ready for longer stories. Illustrations that interpret the story are enticing for children, making these books the ones children will want to have read to them often. Faithfulness to the biblical text is important. You will find such stories in single-story books and in books that contain several stories.

Story Bibles for Children Who Can Read

Before a child is ready to read a "real" Bible, she or he can read from a children's story Bible. These books contain the major stories from the Hebrew Scriptures and the New Testament. Some contain information in the form of a glossary on the page or in the back, maps, and other aids to understanding and thinking about the text. Because these stories are retold, faithfulness to the text is important to check. (You may be surprised how different stories in Scripture can be from the version you learned as a child!)

Children's Bibles

With the many Bible translations available today, you want to look for one that is written in a style and at a reading level understandable to children. Two to consider are the *Common English Bible* (the children's Bible is titled *Deep Blue Bible*) and *Today's English Version*, also known as the *Good News Bible*. Some of these "real" Bibles, which are complete texts, have artwork and study aids that appeal to children. Look for good biblical scholarship, and don't be taken in by fancy packaging.

Resources for Children, Parents, and Families

Resources for Children

Boling, Ruth L., Lauren J. Muzzy, and Laurie A. Vance. *A Children's Guide to Worship*. Louisville, KY: Geneva Press, 1997. This enchanting book introducing the church mice takes you and your child through the service of worship, explaining each part clearly and briefly. A good book to have when your child begins to attend worship, whether part- or full-time.

Boling, Ruth L. *Come Worship with Me: A Journey through the Church Year*. Louisville, KY: Geneva Press, 2000. This beautifully illustrated book features the church mice from *A Children's Guide to Worship* and describes the seasons of the church year as well as many Christian symbols. A helpful accompaniment when you and your child focus on the colors of the church year.

Caldwell, Elizabeth F. and Carol A. Wehrheim. *Growing in God's Love, A Children's Story Bible*. Louisville, KY: Westminster John Knox Press, 2018. One hundred and fifty stories from the Old and New Testaments are retold and illustrated by a variety of artists to engage children visually. Questions are provided for parents and children to talk about the stories.

Levine, Amy-Jill and Sandy Eisenberg Sasso. *Who Counts? 100 Sheep, 10 Coins, and 2 Sons*. Louisville, KY: Westminster John Knox Press, 2017. Three popular parables of Jesus are retold and illustrated with contemporary scenes. The page for parents is a great resource for helping you explain the messages of the parables to your child.

Wehrheim, Carol A. *Baptism Promises*. Louisville, KY: Flyaway Books, 2018. With simple language and charming illustrations, this board book introduces children to the story and day of their baptism.

Resources for Parents

Caldwell, Elizabeth F. *I Wonder: Engaging a Child's Curiosity about the Bible.* Nashville: Abingdon Press, 2016. This book provides solid criteria in selecting a Bible and reading it to and with your child.

Caldwell, Elizabeth F. *Making a Home for Faith: Nurturing the Spiritual Life of Your Children.* Cleveland: Pilgrim Press, 2000. This book explores your role as faith educator and the many ways you can fulfill that role.

Conway, George E. *Giving Good Gifts: The Spiritual Journey of Parenthood.* Louisville, KY: Westminster John Knox Press, 2001. The author identifies seven spiritual gifts parents can give to their children to help them grow into healthy spiritual identities.

McKim, Donald K. *Presbyterian Beliefs: A Brief Introduction, Revised Edition.* Louisville, KY: Westminster John Knox Press, 2017. An easy-to-understand introduction to what Presbyterians believe about major theological questions. A good sourcebook for answering your child's tough questions—and your own!

Miller, Lisa. *The Spiritual Child: The New Science of Parenting for Health and Lifelong Thriving.* New York: St. Martin's Press, 2015. This book describes the importance of developing your child's spiritual life and provides advice about parenting strategies that will help you develop your child's spirituality and your own.

Wehrheim, Carol A. *Giving Together, A Stewardship Guide for Families.* Louisville, KY: Westminster John Knox Press, 2004. Biblical passages support a holistic understanding of stewardship and how families can live their call to be stewards in today's world.

Resources for Families

Glory to God—Hymns and Songs for Children and Families: Singing Faith All Day Long. Louisville, KY: Westminster John Knox Press, 2016. A lovely CD of songs and instrumental music to travel daily with your family, from getting up in the morning to going to bed at night. Play it at home and in the car to introduce your family to music of the faith.

Kirkpatrick, Rebecca. *100 Things Every Child Should Know before Confirmation*. Louisville, KY: Westminster John Knox Press, 2016. This resource highlights one hundred basic facts about the Bible, church history, Christian worship, and world religions, with brief summaries and tips for integrating this knowledge into your child's overall Christian education.